CHILDHOOD FEARS
AND ANXIETIES

SCHOOL FEARS

CHILDHOOD FEARS
AND ANXIETIES

SCHOOL FEARS

H.W. POOLE

SERIES CONSULTANT
ANNE S. WALTERS, Ph.D.

Emma Pendleton Bradley Hospital

Warren Alpert Medical School of
Brown University

MASON CREST

Mason Crest
450 Parkway Drive, Suite D
Broomall, PA 19008
www.masoncrest.com

MTM Publishing, Inc.
435 West 23rd Street, #8C
New York, NY 10011
www.mtmpublishing.com

President: Valerie Tomaselli
Vice President, Book Development: Hilary Poole
Designer: Annemarie Redmond
Copyeditor: Peter Jaskowiak
Editorial Assistant: Leigh Eron

Series ISBN: 978-1-4222-3721-2
Hardback ISBN: 978-1-4222-3729-8
E-Book ISBN: 978-1-4222-8062-1

Library of Congress Cataloging-in-Publication Data
Names: Poole, Hilary W., author.
Title: School fears / by H.W. Poole.
Description: Broomall, PA: Mason Crest, [2017] | Series: Childhood fears and
    anxieties | Includes index.
Identifiers: LCCN 2016053130 (print) | LCCN 2017020018 (ebook) | ISBN
    9781422280621 (ebook) | ISBN 9781422237298 (hardback : alk. paper)
Subjects: LCSH: School phobia—Juvenile literature.
Classification: LCC LB1091 (ebook) | LCC LB1091 .P66 2017 (print) | DDC
    370.15/34—dc23
LC record available at https://lccn.loc.gov/2016053130.

Printed and bound in the United States of America.

First printing
9 8 7 6 5 4 3 2 1

TABLE OF CONTENTS

Key Icons to Look for:

Words to Understand: These words with their easy-to-understand definitions will increase the reader's understanding of the text, while building vocabulary skills.

Sidebars: This boxed material within the main text allows readers to build knowledge, gain insights, explore possibilities, and broaden their perspectives by weaving together additional information to provide realistic and holistic perspectives.

Educational Videos: Readers can view videos by scanning our QR codes, which will provide them with additional educational content to supplement the text. Examples include news coverage, moments in history, speeches, iconic sports moments, and much more.

Text-Dependent Questions: These questions send the reader back to the text for more careful attention to the evidence presented there.

Research Projects: Readers are pointed toward areas of further inquiry connected to each chapter. Suggestions are provided for projects that encourage deeper research and analysis.

Series Glossary of Key Terms: This back-of-the-book glossary contains terminology used throughout the series. Words found here increase the reader's ability to read and comprehend higher-level books and articles in this field.

SERIES INTRODUCTION

Who among us does not have memories of an intense childhood fear? Fears and anxieties are a part of *every* childhood. Indeed, these fears are fodder for urban legends and campfire tales alike. And while the details of these legends and tales change over time, they generally have at their base predictable childhood terrors such as darkness, separation from caretakers, or bodily injury.

We know that fear has an evolutionary component. Infants are helpless, and, compared to other mammals, humans have a very long developmental period. Fear ensures that curious children will stay close to caretakers, making them less likely to be exposed to danger. This means that childhood fears are adaptive, making us more likely to survive, and even thrive, as a species.

Unfortunately, there comes a point when fear and anxiety cease to be useful. This is especially problematic today, for there has been a startling increase in anxiety among children and adolescents. In fact, 25 percent of 13- to 18-year-olds now have mild to moderate anxiety, and the *median* age of onset for anxiety disorders is just 11 years old.

Why might this be? Some say that the contemporary United States is a nation preoccupied with risk, and it is certainly possible that our children are absorbing this preoccupation as well. Certainly, our exposure to potential threats has never been greater. We see graphic images via the media and have more immediate news of all forms of disaster. This can lead our children to feel more vulnerable, and it may increase the likelihood that they respond with fear. If children based their fear on the news that they see on Facebook or on TV, they would dramatically overestimate the likelihood of terrible things happening.

As parents or teachers, what do we do about fear? As in other areas of life, we provide our children with guidance and education on a daily basis. We teach them about the signs and feelings of fear. We discuss and normalize typical fear reactions, and support them in tackling difficult situations despite fear. We explain—and demonstrate by example—how to identify "negative thinking traps" and generate positive coping thoughts instead.

But to do so effectively, we might need to challenge some of our own assumptions about fear. Adults often assume that they must protect their children from fear and help them to avoid scary situations, when sometimes the best course is for the child to face the fear and conquer it. This is counterintuitive for many adults: after all, isn't it our job to reassure our children and help them feel better? Yes, of course! Except when it isn't. Sometimes they need us to help them confront their fears and move forward anyway.

That's where these volumes come in. When it comes to fear, balanced information is critical. Learning about fear as it relates to many different areas can help us to help our children remember that although you don't choose whether to be afraid, you do choose how to handle it. These volumes explore the world of childhood fears, seeking to answer important questions: How much is too much? And how can fear be positive, functioning to mobilize us in the face of danger?

Fear gives us the opportunity to step up and respond with courage and resilience. It pushes us to expand our sphere of functioning to areas that might feel unfamiliar or risky. When we are a little nervous or afraid, we tend to prepare a little more, look for more information, ask more questions—and all of this can function to help us expand the boundaries of our lives in a positive direction. So, while fear might *feel* unpleasant, there is no doubt that it can have a positive outcome.

Let's teach our children that.

—Anne Walters, Ph.D.
Chief Psychologist, Emma Pendleton Bradley Hospital
Clinical Associate Professor,
Alpert Medical School of Brown University

In a perfect world,
every kid would
look forward to
school every day.
Alas, we don't live
in that world.

CHAPTER ONE

BACK TO SCHOOL

There's a TV commercial that used to run every September. Parents are seen dancing through the aisles of stores, as a song declares, "It's the most wonderful time of the year." What time of year do they mean? Back to school, of course.

Parents find that commercial to be pretty funny, but kids . . . not so much. It's very common for kids to feel nervous or downright fearful in the days and weeks before school starts. That's especially true for kids who are starting a new school. Some are making the jump from elementary to middle school, while others moved over the summer and are starting at a totally new school. That's an anxious situation for anyone.

Once school gets under way, there are new things to worry about: keeping up with homework, taking tests, and dealing with teachers, friends, and even bullies. It's a lot, and for some kids, it becomes too much. This book looks at school anxieties and all the different things that can contribute to them.

 WORDS TO UNDERSTAND

conscious: the part of your mind you are aware of, or your active thoughts.

orientation: an introduction to a new place or situation.

subconscious: the part of your mind you are not always aware of, or the things you are thinking about beneath your daily thoughts.

Let's start with that first day of school, which for many kids is the scariest of all.

THE GREAT UNKNOWN

If you have attended your school before and you have friends there, the battle is already half-won. You already know your way around. You know what the cafeteria is like and if you like the food or not. You know what things will look and sound and smell like. Sure, there will be new teachers and a few new kids, but mostly you'll recognize the faces you see when you walk down the hall.

Of course, some things may still worry you. You may not know your teacher or your classroom. You

Making the jump to middle school or junior high can be scary because you may have no idea what to expect.

AM I SICK?

The human brain is a strange organ sometimes. We can feel very worried on a subconscious level (what we sometimes call "the back of our minds,") even though we aren't thinking about it in a conscious way. But even if the worries are at the back of our minds, our bodies still react.

We might have trouble sleeping, but for no specific reason. We might feel "butterflies" in our stomach or have headaches without knowing why. Our palms can get sweaty, and our hearts can start to race. These are all symptoms of anxiety. This situation can be very confusing—your mind is saying "No, I'm not worried about school," but all the while, your body is saying, "Oh yes, you are!"

These symptoms of anxiety are totally normal, and they don't mean you are sick. But you probably do have something bothering you that needs to be addressed. Talk to your parents or another trusted adult about your feelings and when they happen. They can help you figure out the source of your anxiety. That's an important first step toward feeling better.

Worries about what will happen at school tomorrow can make it hard to fall asleep.

might worry about whether your friends will have the same class as you. Also, because each academic year tends to get more challenging, you might worry about whether or not the classes will be too hard. Or maybe you are starting a new activity this year—maybe it's your first year learning a musical instrument or trying out for a particular sport. The point is, even if you know your school pretty well, it's still natural to feel a bit anxious.

And if you *don't* know the school? Then worries can multiply: Will I get lost? Will anyone like me? Is the food terrible?

Whether or not you are a new kid, all these fears boil down to a fear of the unknown. That's a natural human fear—perhaps the most human fear there is. Our anxious brains tend to assume the worst about unfamiliar situations. And the less you know, the more things there are to worry about.

MAKING PLANS

If unknowns are causing anxiety, the way to reduce the anxiety is to reduce the number of unknowns. Of course, you can't figure everything out in advance. But you might be surprised by how much you can do.

For example, it might help to take a tour of the school. Ask to meet your teacher, preferably in the classroom. Find out what path you will take to the bus stop, from the bus to your locker, and then to homeroom. If possible, walk that path once or even several times. Ask to be shown where the bathrooms are, and find out how to get to the cafeteria or gym.

For a lot of kids, middle school is the first time they have to use a real locker with a combination lock; it is also the first time many kids change rooms

EDUCATIONAL VIDEO

Check out this video with advice from teens about dealing with back-to-school anxiety.

Lunchtime can be a source of anxiety for some kids. They might worry about what the food will be like, who they'll sit with, or if they'll have enough time to eat.

for different classes. If those things are worrying you, ask if you can practice using a combination lock, or if you can find out ahead of time how to get from class to class. Some type of orientation like this is usually offered to new kids, but if you don't get the offer, have your parents call and ask.

Even if you are *not* a new kid, don't be ashamed to ask for a visit. Most teachers start setting up their

RESEARCH PROJECT

Ask adults and friends about what they do to reduce anxiety about starting something new. It doesn't have to be school. It could be a new job, or moving to a new town. You can also search online for "back-to-school anxiety" and look for more tips. Using those tips and the ones in this chapter, make a pamphlet that gives younger kids advice on how to make the first day easier. Include advice from your own experience, too!

classrooms before school starts. They would be pleased to have you stop by and meet them. It helps them, too! They want you to start off the year on a good note.

If you are worried about getting to school on time, talk to your family about what your morning ritual will be. If you know what time your bus comes, you can practice getting up, getting dressed, having breakfast, and so on, to make sure you will have enough time. If you are dropped off at school, ask an adult if he or she can do a few "practice runs" so that you know where you are going and how long it will take. Maybe it would help to plan out in advance what you want to wear. Put all your school supplies into your backpack, so that you can feel confident nothing has been forgotten. Do you have your own alarm clock? (If not, ask for one!) Start setting the alarm and take charge of making sure you get up on time.

The point is, don't just sit and worry—turn your worries into action. This accomplishes two things. First, it's good to be prepared so that you don't get lost or forget something important. Second, and more important, the very act of anticipating a problem and taking steps to avoid it will make you feel more confident.

One last piece of advice: don't overlook practical things like having a good breakfast and getting enough sleep. Most kids stay up a lot later during the summer than they do during the school year. It is a

smart idea to start getting back into a routine *before* school actually starts. Experts recommend getting yourself on a school schedule about a week before school. It sounds boring, but if you have not eaten or slept, you are just not going to feel very good no matter what else you do!

An alarm clock can help reduce anxiety about getting to school on time.

TEXT-DEPENDENT QUESTIONS

1. What is the main cause of back-to-school worries?

2. What are the types of things that make some kids anxious?

3. What can be done to reduce those anxieties?

Scary teachers can be a cause of school anxiety.

CHAPTER TWO

TEACHERS AND TESTS

When your parents were in school, kindergarten mostly involved finger painting, playing with blocks, and naps. Reading wasn't considered something kindergarteners were supposed to learn. Things have changed a lot! These days, many schools tell parents that their kids should be reading before kindergarten even starts.

This emphasis on early achievement has added to school anxiety. Of course, kids have worried about school ever since school was invented. But today, they are more worried, and at younger ages, than ever before. "Things have changed dramatically with my students over the past couple of decades," Dr. Sharon Sevier told *The Atlantic* magazine. "The competition and pressure on kids have really increased . . . . School is more challenging, the stakes seem to be higher."

TEST ANXIETY

One of the big sources of anxiety is taking tests. It's understandable why you might feel nervous before

WORDS TO UNDERSTAND

motivating: something that makes you want to work harder.

paralyzing: something that makes you unable to move (can refer to physical movement as well as emotions).

perception: the way things *appear*, but not necessarily how they *are*.

phobia: an extreme fear of a specific thing.

taking a test. By definition, a *test* is an activity meant to determine whether or not you can do something. It's natural to feel nervous about being judged. But for many kids, their worry about tests goes far beyond simple nervousness. Some get stomachaches or headaches, others start to sweat or feel dizzy. These are physical symptoms of stress.

Test anxiety can also cause emotional reactions. You might feel angry or scared. You could feel helpless or disappointed in yourself before the test even starts. A big problem with test anxiety is that all these bad feelings can actually mess up your thought process, making the test seem harder than it actually is. People with severe test anxiety have trouble concentrating. Their anxiety can even make them doubt answers that they know deep down are correct.

Everybody is different, but we can identify a few general causes of test anxiety. Not all of these apply to every person.

First, and probably most important, is the fear of failure. For some people, the idea that they might fail is motivating—in other words, the desire to avoid failure inspires them to work harder. But for other people, the idea that they could fail is paralyzing. They think that if they get a bad grade, that means that somehow they *are* bad. The fear that they won't succeed becomes so great that they can't act at all. This is ironic, because feeling this much anxiety about failure almost guarantees it will happen.

Another cause of test anxiety is the fear that you don't know enough or have the right skills to succeed. Sometimes this is because you haven't studied enough. Or maybe you are worried that you have studied the wrong things. Some kids are just hard on themselves; they feel that they could never do *enough* to prepare.

Another cause of test anxiety is the simple fact that some kids struggle with certain subjects. And some kids have learning disorders. For students with such issues, taking a test is likely to mean extra pressure.

Finally, some people have a bad experience with a test and then assume that every experience will be that bad or even worse. Their memories about one test curdle into a phobia about every test. Each difficult experience piles on to the next one.

An increase in so-called standardized tests has been matched by an increase in anxiety among many kids.

DEALING WITH TESTS

Unfortunately, tests are a part of life. Certainly they are unavoidable in school, and even outside school, there are tests occasionally. So, since we can't get away from tests, here are some tips for dealing with them:

- **Talk to your teacher or a counselor about your worries.** If you have been diagnosed with a learning disability, find out if there are any special plans that can be made to help you. Sometimes a teacher might let you see a sample test ahead of time. Not one with the same questions, of course! But an old test from an earlier year that is similar to the one you'll take. You can use these practice tests to get a feel for how the actual test will go—look at the instructions carefully, read the questions and make sure you understand what is asked of you in each one. This will take some of the fear of the unknown away.

- **Be prepared.** Of course, "prepared" means studying, but not only that. Find out where and when you are taking the test. Do you need particular pencils or other supplies? Is it the type of tests where you can bring notes with you? The more you know about what the test will be like, the less uncertainty you will have. And the less uncertainty you have, the calmer you will feel.

EDUCATIONAL VIDEO

Check out this video with advice about test anxiety.

- **Read instructions slowly and carefully.** You'd be surprised how often people have a hard time with a test just because they don't understand what is being asked of them. Ask for more explanation if you need to.
- **Stay focused.** If your mind wanders to other topics, gently bring your attention back to the test in front of you. Remind yourself that there will be lots of time to think about other things once the test is over.

Unfortunately, having test anxiety can make it harder to do well on tests, because when people are stressed out, they often have trouble thinking clearly.

FEAR OF TEACHERS

Teachers are authority figures. With the exception of parents, teachers are the main authority figures that kids have to deal with. In fact, it's not uncommon for kids to spend more waking hours at school among teachers than they do with their parents. So the relationships that kids have with their teachers are very important.

When you're a kid, teachers often seem to exist in their own universe, somehow apart from the rest of us. But that's just your perception. Teachers are regular humans, with cars and pets and houses and—oftentimes—kids of their own.

This means they have good days and bad days, just like us. And teachers can get frustrated, just like us. When you think a teacher is being mean, try to imagine what his or her life is like. Do students misbehave or argue frequently? That may be the source of the teacher's "meanness." For example,

Everybody is different—your least-favorite teacher is some other kid's most-favorite.

THE MOST IMPORTANT THING

The most important thing to remember about school is this: *teachers and administrators want you to succeed.* Sometimes it may not feel that way. Teachers get busy and stressed out, coaches yell a lot, and so on. It may seem like principals and vice principals exist only to lecture and punish you. You might think that all adults are against you and your friends.

But those adults have devoted their whole lives to education. They do it because they believe in students, and they want you to do well.

So when you feel nervous or afraid, remember that it's okay to ask for help. Teachers and administrators are on your side. And yes, maybe certain people might seem grumpy or disinterested at times. (Everybody has bad days.) But don't give up. There is somebody at your school, *right now*, who wants to help you.

maybe the teacher really loves the particular book she is teaching that day, but the entire class looks bored. Instead of thinking of your teacher as an all-powerful scary person, maybe she's just another fellow human having a bad day.

Also, keep in mind that there are all kinds of people in the world. Sometimes a particular teaching style suits one kid but not another. The problem of "mean teachers" is often a question of mismatched personalities. It might seem impossible, but your Worst Teacher is some other kid's Favorite Teacher.

Every once in a while, though, there are real problems in the class. If so, talk to your parents or some other trusted adult about the situation.

Ask a teacher at your school if he or she is willing to be interviewed. If you are really brave, pick a teacher who you find a bit scary; if that's too much, pick a teacher you like. Ask about why he or she wanted to become a teacher and what it was like to study education. Find out what the teacher does to prepare for class before and after school. Ask what the teacher remembers about the people who taught him or her. Take good notes during your conversation and write up a profile of the teacher. What did you learn from your conversation?

Be ready to share examples of things the teacher said or did. Try to be as specific as you can. Adults need to know *exactly* what the problem is. It's not enough to say, "my teacher is scary," which could mean almost anything.

Your parent or guardian may need to take your concerns to the school counselor or principal. That's why it's so important that you give specific examples of what you feel is wrong. Your parent will need to explain the issue to the administrators to figure out how to fix it.

GENERAL FEAR OF TEACHERS

Sometimes kids don't find just one teacher scary, but all of them. For these kids, any interaction with authority figures is stressful. They feel panicked and upset, even if the teacher in question is really nice. This can be a big problem, since asking questions in class is an important part of learning. If you are afraid to talk to your teachers at all, that's going to get in the way of your education.

It's important to remember that these panicky feelings are part of our "fight-or-flight" response, which is a natural human reaction to threats. It's wired deep into our brains and is not going to go away. The problem is that your math teacher is unlikely to pose any real danger to you. So feeling panicky around a teacher isn't helpful.

People become teachers because they love kids and they love learning.

You might try practicing what you want to say to the teacher in advance. Let's imagine that you have a particular question about math, and you know you have to ask for help, but you are afraid to. Role-play the situation with a parent or sibling, where the other person pretends to be the teacher. You can also write out your problem in advance. Sometimes having things written down can make the in-person conversation easier. For more on this topic, see the volume *Social Fears* in this set.

 TEXT-DEPENDENT QUESTIONS

1. What are some reasons people feel anxious about tests?

2. What are some things they can do to feel less nervous?

3. What are some tips for getting over a fear of teachers?

Dealing with other kids can be a huge source of school anxiety.

CHAPTER THREE

FRIENDS AND OTHERS

There's much more to school than teachers and tests. In fact, for most kids, teachers and tests are not nearly as important as friendships. Unfortunately, dealing with peers can also be one of the more stressful aspects of school.

MAKING FRIENDS

Some people find it easy to have conversations with strangers. But for most of us, interacting with people we don't know can be stressful. Meeting people and making new friends is not easy for everyone. Here are some things you can do to make it easier:

- **Try to be patient.** First, always remember that it takes time to make friends. If you are in a new class or new school, try not to expect to make friends instantly. Friendships develop over time: one conversation here, another conversation there. So don't be hard on yourself if it takes a little while.

 WORDS TO UNDERSTAND

empathy: the ability to understand how someone else feels.

harassment: picking on another person frequently and deliberately.

peers: people who are roughly the same age as you.

Being "popular" at school is not nearly as important as having a close friend who really understands you.

- **Try to be open.** Kids are still figuring out who they are. And most of them are just as nervous as you. Try not to assume that particular people can't be your friends because of how they look or act. First impressions can be deceiving. There's no way to know what people are really like until you have gotten to know them. Give them a chance.

- **Try to relax.** Sometimes people try so hard to make friends or impress others that they end up having the opposite effect. You don't have to show off for people to like you. If you are a shy person, the thought of making a mistake in front of strangers might make you anxious.

Try to set those worries aside and ignore them. Here's a secret: other people are much more focused on their own insecurities than they are on yours. They almost never judge you as much as you assume.

- **Try to be realistic.** Friendship is not a competition, and there's no prize for having the largest number of friends. If you have lots of friends, that's great! But all you really need are one or two buddies who understand you.
- **Try to take the long view.** There can be a lot of conflicts between kids at school: he said X, she said Y, and so on. Some people refer to it as "drama," and sometimes it

Drama between friends is really common in middle school.

seems the drama will never end. Here's something to keep in mind: drama seems like a huge deal when you are in the middle of it, but it will be forgotten in a few days or weeks. (There will be some other drama by then!) When drama is getting you down, see if you can step away from it. Try to take your mind off it by focusing on an activity you enjoy that has nothing to do with your relationships at school. Taking a mini-vacation from the drama will help you refocus on what really matters. Your time in school feels long, but it is actually a very short phase of a long life.

DEALING WITH BULLIES

Of course, sometimes problems can't be written off as just drama. Sometimes kids have real conflicts that need to be addressed in a serious way. Maybe there is another kid or kids whom you absolutely cannot get along with for some reason. Maybe other kids are ganging up because there is something different about you, and they won't leave you alone. It might not even be happening at school—sometimes these problems occur online instead. These can be really tough situations, and you may need to get some adult help.

Bullying is when one person or a group of people targets another person or group for regular

EDUCATIONAL VIDEO

Check out this video for advice about bullying.

harassment. The classic bullying situation is a bigger kid taking the lunch money of a smaller kid, but these days bullying is just as likely to happen online. Sometimes people spread rumors about others or post embarrassing pictures. But no matter where it happens, bullying causes huge amounts of anxiety for its victims. It's *very* hard to be the target of a

The most visible type of bullying is physical, but bullying can be emotional as well.

bully. It can make you feel helpless and that nobody will understand.

Fortunately there is a lot more awareness of bullying than there used to be. Here are some quick tips on dealing with bullies:

- **If possible, don't respond.** Bullies are often trying to make you react, because controlling you makes them feel important. If you can (and you can't always), try to ignore their insults. Bullies tend to get easily bored, and they are likely to move on if they can't get a reaction out of you.

- **There is safety in numbers.** Stick up for other people being bullied, just as they should stick up for you.

Sometimes it seems like new technologies just give kids new ways to pick on each other.

RESOURCES ON BULLYING

Here are some websites with information about bullying:

*   Stopbullying.gov. A site hosted by the U.S. Department of Health and Human Services, with lots of great resources for kids, parents, and teachers.
*   It Gets Better Project (www.itgetsbetter.org). Videos and information about bulling for LGBTQ kids.
*   KidsHealth: Dealing with Bullying (http://kidshealth.org/en/teens/bullies.html). An overview of bullying, with advice about what to do.

*   **Ask for help.** You might think that adults can't understand what you are going through. But the truth is, lots of adults remember being bullied, and they can help you figure out ways to respond. Talk to your parent or some other trusted adult, such as a teacher, coach, or someone from your church. And if the first adult you approach doesn't help, don't give up! There is somebody out there who will understand your situation, so keep asking. (There are some online sources in the sidebar on this page that you could also try.)

WAIT . . . AM I THE BULLY?

Do you ever call people names that you know will hurt or upset them? Do you shove kids who are

RESEARCH PROJECT

Take the Bullying Survey put out by the Southern Poverty Law Center (www.tolerance.org/lesson/bullying-survey), and ask people you know to take it as well. The instructions are written for classrooms, but you could use the same survey among your friends and family. How many people have been called names, or mistreated? How many have seen it happen to others? How many have done those things themselves? Are there more bullies or victims in your survey?

weaker than you? Or threaten somebody because you want to scare them? Maybe you'd never do things like that in real life—but do you say mean stuff on social media?

Give some thought to why you do these things. It probably seemed like you had a good reason at the time. For example, maybe you had a lousy morning and it put you in a bad mood, and then when you got to school, some kid got in your way or annoyed you, and so you lashed out. Maybe you tell yourself that things you say online don't really matter, or maybe you're trying to be funny and impress somebody else. Maybe there's one kid who just really gets on your nerves for reasons you can't explain.

You're only human, and it's understandable to feel angry or irritated. Especially when you're in front of a keyboard, it can seem like there's no harm in just expressing whatever's on your mind (or seems funny) at the time. But the thing is, hurting others does not make anything better. Making others feel bad will not fix whatever is bad about your own situation.

Talk to an adult you trust about what's making you want to insult, shove, or mock others. Also, try to find some empathy for people you dislike. After all, would you want to be insulted, shoved, or hurt? Would you be okay if you went online and saw a bunch of insults directed at you? Probably not.

None of us are going to like every single person we meet. But you *can* choose to "live and let live," rather than hurt people who are different from you or weaker than you are.

Saying mean stuff about people on social media can be a form of bullying. Think how you'd feel if it happened to you.

 TEXT-DEPENDENT QUESTIONS

1. What are some tips for making new friends?

2. Where does bullying happen?

3. What are some tips for responding to bullying?

It's important to face your fears, so that *you* are in charge of your life, not your anxiety.

CHAPTER FOUR

BEATING ANXIETY

Sometimes we know exactly what is making us feel worried. But a lot of times, we aren't sure exactly why we feel so anxious. We have a vague sense of dread—a sinking feeling in our stomachs that won't go away—but we aren't sure why. A lot of the advice in this book revolves around facing your worries head on, but that's pretty tough to do if you aren't sure exactly why you feel that way.

THE WORRY LIST

Here is an exercise that may help. Get a pencil and paper, and write a list of all the bad things that *could* happen at school. Don't judge the ideas you have, just brainstorm. If you have trouble getting started, try writing the craziest things you can think up, like your school being hit by an asteroid, or sharks in the bathroom. Then move your thoughts toward real-life problems. You could miss the bus, your school clothes could be totally wrong, or a mean kid might

WORDS TO UNDERSTAND

achievable: reasonably doable.

panic attack: an episode of intense fear, usually for no obvious reason.

vital: extremely important.

bug you. Just keep writing things down—it doesn't matter if they are silly or weird.

When you have totally run out of ideas, read through your list from the beginning. What items on the list *truly* worry you? Circle those things. Let's say one is "I could miss the bus." The next step is to brainstorm some things you could do to prevent the bad thing from happening. (Some bad things are not preventable, but others are.) Certainly you can take some actions to avoid missing the bus. Write down what makes sense in your situation. For example, you might write, "Get up 10 minutes earlier," or "Plan my clothes the night before, to save time." Next, write down ideas of what you'll do if the bad thing happens anyway. It might be: "Ask Mom to drive me," or "Call my grandmother for a ride." Finally, write down what may happen as a result of this problem. Write down the worst (but realistic) things you can think of, like, "Major embarrassment due to walking in late," or "Tardy on my record." Look at those worst-case ideas carefully. How bad are they, really? Are they worth having stomachaches or losing sleep over? Many times they are not! You may realize that what is worrying you is not so terrible after all.

The next step is to talk to an adult you trust about your list. Make sure that the steps you are planning are smart and achievable. Then put the best plans into practice. In other words, don't just imagine what you *might* do—actually *do* the things you imagine!

And now you deserve a round of applause, because you have done something really cool. You have looked your fear straight in the eye. You now know a lot more about your anxiety than you did before. You are now in charge, rather than your fears being in charge of you.

Talk to an adult about your Worry List, and try to come up with concrete things you can do in order to shrink the number of things you worry about.

SCHOOL REFUSAL

Unfortunately, not all anxiety can be conquered with a list. Sometimes, severe anxiety can result in something called "school refusal." School refusal is pretty much what it sounds like: kids feel so much anxiety about school that they don't want to go anymore. Or sometimes kids get to school, but then they want to be sent home right away. Some kids develop bad stomachaches or headaches when they even *think* about going to school. Other kids get angry or throw tantrums if they are forced to go.

School refusal is a problem for a few different reasons. First, when you don't go to school, you aren't learning the things that all your peers are learning. The longer you stay out, the harder it will be to catch up.

But classwork is just one part of the problem with school refusal. School is actually not just about learning math or history; it is also about learning how to get along in the world. Making friends, solving problems, learning to work as a team—these are all vital experiences for every person. Skipping school doesn't just mean skipping algebra, but it means skipping out on all that social stuff, too.

Here's another problem. If you skip school *just* because of the anxiety you feel, then your anxiety is in charge. But your life should not be defined by anxiety. Anxiety is just a feeling—it is not who you are.

For kids with really strong anxiety, just getting on the bus can be really tough.

THE BAD PARTS

This may sound weird, but one aspect of going to school is learning how to deal with the parts of each day that are no fun at all. Of course, we all want school to be totally interesting and fun all the time. It isn't, but that's because nothing is!

Even the most awesome jobs have bad parts. Movie stars have to learn lines, for instance; also they spend tons of time waiting around for the next scene to be ready. Sports stars have to run different kinds of drills, where they practice the same skill over and over again. Musicians sit in recording studios, working on some tiny bit of a song for hours, trying to get it just right. Everybody, no matter how cool their lives might look, has frustrations and annoyances at work. The way they overcome those frustrations can be the difference between being just okay at their jobs and being great at them.

Experts say that school refusal is usually a symptom of some other problem that needs attention. For example, a problem with bullying might result in school refusal. Changing schools can cause a lot of anxiety that makes some kids refuse school. Fear of failure can cause school refusal, as can the fear that something bad will happen to a parent or sibling while the kid is at school. In order to fix the problem of school refusal, parents—often with the help of a doctor or therapist—need to help kids figure out what is truly bothering them.

Once that main problem is addressed, then kids can start returning to school. Frequently, kids who are trying to get over school refusal will attend school for

Your teachers really do want to help you deal with your anxiety.

EDUCATIONAL VIDEO

Check out this video about generalized anxiety disorder.

very short periods at first, and then slowly increase the amount of time they spend in the school building.

ANXIETY DISORDERS

If you catch a cold, you'll probably stay home from school for a day or two until you feel better. Then you'll go back to school and everything will return to normal. But if you have an anxiety disorder, things are a little more complicated.

Anxiety disorders are defined by a book that doctors use called the *Diagnostic and Statistical Manual of Mental Disorders* (*DSM*). There are a bunch of different types of disorders, including generalized anxiety disorder, social anxiety, panic disorder, and more. Some people with anxiety disorders feel anxiety all the time, but for no clear reason. Others feel anxiety only in particular situations. Some have a phobia about public speaking, for example, which makes it very hard to participate in class. Some people with anxiety disorders have panic attacks, while others don't. But all anxiety disorders boil down to the same basic idea: an anxiety disorder is when you feel so much anxiety that you have trouble participating in regular daily activities.

If you have an anxiety disorder, you are not alone. The National Institute of Mental Health estimates that one in four teenagers will face an anxiety disorder at some point. Anxiety disorders are different from physical illnesses in certain ways. There's no magic pill that can make an anxiety disorder go away. There are medications that can help, but people with anxiety disorders almost always have to learn how to manage their disorder in other ways, too. They learn what to do when anxious feelings arise, so they stay in control of their lives. For much more on anxiety disorders and what can be done about them, you might read another title in this set, *Symptoms and Treatments of Anxiety Disorders.*

RESEARCH PROJECT

Research the different types of anxiety disorders and write a report on the one you find most interesting. What are the symptoms of this specific disorder, and what makes it different from other types of anxiety? How is the disorder treated?

TEXT-DEPENDENT QUESTIONS

1. What are some things to keep in mind when making new friends?

2. What's a Worry List and how might it help with school anxiety?

3. What is the difference between typical anxiety and an anxiety disorder?

FURTHER READING

Anxiety and Depression Association of America. "School Refusal." https://www.adaa.org/living-with-anxiety/children/school-refusal.

AnxietyBC. "Coping With Back to School Anxiety." https://www.anxietybc.com/parenting/coping-back-school-anxiety.

Coloroso, Barbara. *The Bully, the Bullied, and the Bystander.* Updated ed. New York: HarperCollins, 2008.

Dwyer, Lucy. "When Anxiety Hits at School." *The Atlantic*, October 3, 2014. http://www.theatlantic.com/health/archive/2014/10/when-anxiety-hits-at-school/380622/.

Ehmke, Rachel. "Anxiety in the Classroom." Child Mind Institute. http://childmind.org/article/anxiety-in-the-classroom/.

Ehmke, Rachel. "Tips for Beating Test Anxiety." Child Mind Institute. http://childmind.org/article/tips-for-beating-test-anxiety/.

Schab, Lisa. *The Anxiety Workbook for Teens.* Oakland, CA: New Harbinger, 2008.

EDUCATIONAL VIDEOS

Chapter One: Melanie Murphy. "Back to School Anxiety and Advice with Theodora Lee!" https://youtu.be/ChngxDSkQZI.

Chapter Two: AsapThought. "7 Tips to Beat Test Anxiety." https://youtu.be/FyBdA61GmJ0.

Chapter Three: Joey Graceffa. "Bullying Advice!" https://youtu.be/EHz-2qHJk_Y.

Chapter Four: Howcast. "What is Generalized Anxiety Disorder?" https://youtu.be/pDDrt6YiFNU.

SERIES GLOSSARY

adaptive: a helpful response to a particular situation.

bias: a feeling against a particular thing or idea.

biofeedback: monitoring of bodily functions with the goal of learning to control those functions.

cognitive: relating to the brain and thought.

comorbid: when one illness or disorder is present alongside another one.

context: the larger situation in which an event takes place.

diagnose: to identify an illness or disorder.

exposure: having contact with something.

extrovert: a person who enjoys being with others.

harassment: picking on another person frequently and deliberately.

hypnosis: creating a state of consciousness where someone is awake but highly open to suggestion.

inhibitions: feelings that restricts what we do or say.

introvert: a person who prefers being alone.

irrational: baseless; something that's not connected to reality.

melatonin: a substance that helps the body regulate sleep.

milestone: an event that marks a stage in development.

motivating: something that makes you want to work harder.

occasional: from time to time; not often.

panic attack: sudden episode of intense, overwhelming fear.

paralyzing: something that makes you unable to move (can refer to physical movement as well as emotions).

peers: people who are roughly the same age as you.

perception: what we see and believe to be true.

persistent: continuing for a noticeable period.

phobia: extreme fear of a particular thing.

preventive: keeping something from happening.

probability: the likelihood that a particular thing will happen.

psychological: having to do with the mind and thoughts.

rational: based on a calm understanding of facts, rather than emotion.

sedative: a type of drug that slows down bodily processes, making people feel relaxed or even sleepy.

self-conscious: overly aware of yourself, to the point that it makes you awkward.

serotonin: a chemical in the brain that is important in moods.

stereotype: an oversimplified idea about a type of person that may not be true for any given individual.

stigma: a sense of shame or disgrace associated with a particular state of being.

stimulant: a group of substances that speed up bodily processes.

subconscious: thoughts and feelings you have but may not be aware of.

syndrome: a condition.

treatable: describes a medical condition that can be healed.

upheaval: a period of great change or uncertainty.

INDEX

ABOUT THE ADVISOR

Anne S. Walters is Clinical Associate Professor of Psychiatry and Human Behavior at the Alpert Medical School of Brown University. She is also Chief Psychologist for Bradley Hospital. She is actively involved in teaching activities within the Clinical Psychology Training Programs of the Alpert Medical School and serves as Child Track Seminar Co-Coordinator. Dr. Walters completed her undergraduate work at Duke University, graduate school at Georgia State University, internship at UTexas Health Science Center, and postdoctoral fellowship at Brown University.

ABOUT THE AUTHOR

H. W. Poole is a writer and editor of books for young people, including the sets, *Families Today* and *Mental Illnesses and Disorders: Awareness and Understanding* (Mason Crest). She created the *Horrors of History* series (Charlesbridge) and the *Ecosystems* series (Facts On File). She has also been responsible for many critically acclaimed reference books, including *Political Handbook of the World* (CQ Press) and the *Encyclopedia of Terrorism* (SAGE). She was coauthor and editor of *The History of the Internet* (ABC-CLIO), which won the 2000 American Library Association RUSA award.

PHOTO CREDITS